FINANCING AND CONDUCTING

A POLITICAL CAMPAIGN

Corona Brezina

New York

Published in 2020 by The Rosen Publishing Group, Inc.
29 East 21st Street, New York, NY 10010

Library of Congress Cataloging-in-Publication Data

Names: Brezina, Corona, author.
Title: Financing and conducting a political campaign / Corona Brezina.
Description: New York : Rosen Publishing, 2020 | Series: Be the change!
: political participation in your community | Includes bibliographical
references and index. | Audience: Grade 7 to 12.
Identifiers: LCCN 2019008483| ISBN 9781725340817
(library bound) | ISBN 9781725340800 (pbk.)
Subjects: LCSH: Political campaigns—United States—Juvenile
literature. | Campaign management—United States—Juvenile literature.
| Campaign funds—United States—Juvenile literature.
Classification: LCC JK2281 .B73 2019 | DDC 324.70973—dc23
LC record available at https://lccn.loc.gov/2019008483

Manufactured in the United States of America

CONTENTS

INTRODUCTION

In 2016, college administrator and single mother Letitia Clark ran for city council in Tustin, California. She hired an experienced campaign manager and began making appearances to ask for her constituents' votes. Her family and friends helped out with donations and personal support. Despite being an underdog candidate, her campaign raised twice as much money as she expected.

"I wanted to serve, I wanted to volunteer," Clark told Slate. "I wanted to make a difference for some groups."

In November of that year, she won the city council seat.

Running for local government is a great move for a community member who feels called to service. Some candidates are motivated by a desire to change the system or give back to the community. Others are compelled by a passion for a specific issue. Staff and volunteers join a campaign when they believe in a candidate's message and want to help that person win the election.

There's a saying that "all politics is local," meaning that elected officials should not neglect the key issues that affect their constituents. Local government comprises a wide range of positions, such as mayor, city council, clerk, treasurer, school board, library board, prosecutor, and sheriff. Additional offices

Before being elected a representative for Minnesota in the US House of Representatives in 2018, Ilhan Omar gained experience managing campaigns for other candidates and serving as a Minnesota House representative.

include county commissioners, judges, property assessors, and offices in special districts that provide a specific service, such as conservation districts or sanitary districts. Types of governments vary from one city or town to another. In some, there may be a wide variety of elected offices; in others, some positions may be appointed rather than elected. Offices can be either partisan—meaning candidates declare a political party—or nonpartisan.

Campaigning for political office is an intense and demanding process. Candidates must have people skills and organizational skills. They must understand campaign laws and financing operations. The candidate must be aware of the issues that voters care about and have a message that appeals to them. Communication skills of all types are essential—in-person, on the phone, in writing, and online. The candidate should be able to hold a crowd's attention during a speech and persuade a skeptical voter during door-to-door canvassing.

Campaign staff and volunteers help spread the candidate's message and get out the vote. Working on a political campaign can be a rewarding experience for everyone involved, from old hands on the trail to high school students volunteering on their first campaign. Political participation is an opportunity to achieve change in the community and gain valuable skills and experience along the way.

LAYING THE GROUNDWORK

When a nationally known politician announces a run for a high office such as president or senator, the event is often a major news story. Commentators analyze the content and tone of the announcement speech. They review the candidate's record, identifying assets and liabilities that may affect voters' perceptions. Political opponents pounce with attempts to discredit the candidate.

Candidates for a local political office won't attract such close scrutiny, but it's nonetheless vital that they conduct a savvy and comprehensive campaign. A potential candidate should be highly organized and conform to campaign laws and regulations from the earliest stages—a chaotic campaign or apparent incompetence will make a bad impression on voters.

EXPLORING OPTIONS

Before deciding to run for office, prospective candidates should weigh their political ambitions and assess whether they're achievable. There are many different factors that can impel political involvement. Some people are naturally drawn to public service and participation in the political process. They may have family members who work in government, or they may have grown up in a politically engaged household. A candidate may be driven by a single issue, such as school reform. Some candidates may be motivated by the desire to bring about positive change in their community.

A candidate may enter the race primarily out of a desire to address local or community concerns or out of dissatisfaction with the incumbent's performance. Others view local office as a first step to higher elected office or position in government.

Often, candidates are actively recruited to run for office. Supporters may urge qualified individuals to consider becoming candidates. Political parties, activist groups, and community organizations also recruit candidates who otherwise may not have considered the idea of running. Sometimes, an elected official may suggest that a campaign staff

For some people, political involvement begins with community activism. Here, demonstrators protest a proposed gas pipeline that would be constructed close to residential neighborhoods and a nuclear power plant.

member run for office. On a local level, a community organization might try to recruit a local business leader known for supporting causes important to residents and institutions. A county board member might urge an involved and well-informed citizen to consider running for the board of commissioners.

The people and groups who recruit candidates take into consideration an individual's qualifications and ideology as well as other factors. They may be impressed by someone's business and social connections, organizational experience, leadership abilities, or specific expertise. They also look for candidates whose policy views match their own. Some organizations may focus on recruiting a diverse range of candidates, aiming to increase representation of women, minorities, and young people in government roles.

Potential candidates may be reluctant to consider running for office. Some qualified individuals hold negative opinions of the political system and government institutions. They may be uncomfortable with the public scrutiny and loss of privacy involved in running for office. The media and political opponents may delve into a candidate's personal as well as professional background for news scoops or smear campaigns that will harm the candidate's reputation. A political campaign requires personal investment of both time and money. Candidates may also worry about how embarking on a political campaign could affect their family life or other career goals.

Before considering a run for office, prospective candidates should check out the local political landscape. They should research the demographics

A Texas congressman examines maps showing state voting districts. Statistics from past elections can help potential candidates determine whether voters are likely to support their bid for office.

and voting patterns in the district. At this stage, candidates should consider whether they are running for the right office. If there's no realistic chance of winning, it might be sensible to consider running for a different position rather than pursue a long-shot campaign.

A candidate can learn about voting trends in the district by examining past election results. Voter turnout numbers can reveal an approximate number of votes needed for victory. Election results also indicate the political leanings of voters. In strongly Republican or Democratic districts, the incumbent of the majority party is often heavily favored to win.

DOING THE MATH

When considering a run for office, prospective candidates should draw up a rough budget to estimate how much money they would need to raise in order to run a viable campaign. According to Dick Simpson and Betty O'Shaughnessy's *Winning Elections in the 21st Century*, a campaign for local office relying on volunteers may cost a few thousand dollars. A competitive race in a big city might cost a few hundred thousand dollars. Many factors impact how much money a candidate will need to spend. These factors include the population and political makeup of the district. Candidates will need to spend more to win over constituents if most of the people in their district generally support the opposing party.

Basic campaign costs are likely to include rent for a campaign office, staff salaries, advertisements, campaign mailings, fundraising expenses, a website, campaign materials (such as yard signs and flyers), office supplies, and various filing fees. One of the biggest costs will be mailings and postage. Candidates can estimate the expense by considering how many voters in the district they will target.

Candidates should also do some preliminary opposition research—learning about the other candidates in the race. In national races, opposition research focuses on gathering information that might discredit opponents. In a local race, candidates should assess the strengths of the incumbent and other potential opponents and identify campaign issues likely to be important in the race. They should also talk to community leaders, experienced campaigners, and officeholders in the district to assess voters' priorities, discuss tactics, and gauge whether the candidate has a reasonable chance of winning.

DECLARING CANDIDACY

A candidate should be familiar with the requirements for the office before running. The laws vary widely from one state or city to another. There is often a minimum age requirement for public office. In general, states and cities require that candidates be at least twenty-five years old.

There are exceptions, though. For example, in 2018, six teenagers filed to run for governor of Kansas, as reported by CNN. At the time, the state of Kansas did not have any age requirements for officeholders.

Teen politicians are occasionally elected to local public office, such as mayor or city council, in places with no age requirements. Some towns and cities encourage civic engagement by young people through teen city councils or youth councils.

Most districts require that candidates be US citizens and meet residency requirements. Usually, candidates must live in the city or district of the office they're running for, and in some cities, they must have been a resident for at least a certain number of years. They must also be registered to vote at an address in their district.

Certain factors may disqualify candidates from running for local office. Some cities may prohibit individuals from holding a certain office if they also have business dealings with city government. In other places, officials who do business with the city can hold public office as long as they recuse themselves

Eighteen-year-old candidate Edward Burroughs campaigns for a school board seat in Temple Hills, Maryland. He won the seat, becoming Maryland's youngest elected state official.

(withdraw from participating) when there may be a conflict of interest. People with certain criminal convictions are also sometimes barred from running for office. For some offices, prior experience, training, or education may be required or highly recommended. These range from county sheriffs to judges to seats on specialized boards, such as soil and water conservation districts.

Depending on the office, officially declaring candidacy can either be a low-key matter of asking for endorsement from a local political party organization, or it can be a carefully scripted publicity event.

Regardless of the setting, the announcement is the candidate's chance to make a good first impression on voters.

The candidate should begin assembling a campaign organization and obtaining the endorsement of local politicians and community leaders ahead of any formal announcement. Candidates who have been actively recruited by supporters or political players have the advantage of a preexisting support base for their campaign. One of the first jobs for the team is to organize the official announcement. They will consider details such as the location and date. They will help craft a message for the announcement, notify the local media, issue a press release, and prepare campaign literature to hand out. They'll also encourage supporters to attend to generate excitement about the campaign.

GETTING ON THE BALLOT

In addition to wooing the public, the candidate must navigate paperwork and the fine details of election law. Mistakes regarding filing requirements and deadlines can result in a candidacy being challenged. A city clerk or elections official can provide a manual for candidates along with other materials such as voter files and a calendar with official deadlines. The internet and public library can also be a useful source of information on election laws and financial disclosure requirements.

For some offices, a candidate must submit a petition with a certain number of signatures. Volunteers and staff organize a nominating petition drive to collect signatures from registered voters in the district.

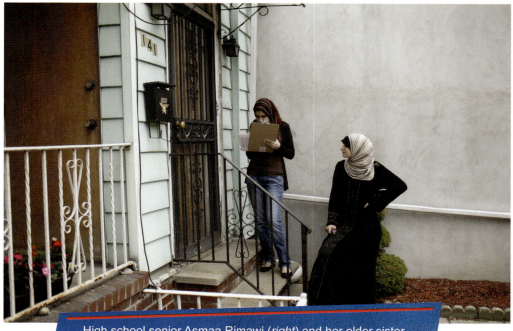

High school senior Asmaa Rimawi (*right*) and her older sister Fatimah collect signatures during a petition drive for Democratic Party candidates in Brooklyn, New York.

In addition to fulfilling a formal requirement, the nominating petition drive gives the campaign a chance to raise awareness of the candidate among voters and connect with potential donors or volunteers.

A candidate should aim to file more than the required number of signatures and submit them before the deadline in case any of the entries are challenged. If there's early controversy over whether or not a candidate fulfills the requirements to be on the ballot, the dispute could stick in voters' minds throughout the election season.

CHAPTER TWO

BEHIND THE SCENES

Every candidate is supported by a dedicated team of staff and volunteers who do the stump work. A candidate for a local office, such as a seat on the school board of a town, may recruit just a handful of part-time volunteers; a candidate for a position such as a council seat of a larger city may hire several full-time staff members with expertise in campaigning. A great team will include both experienced campaigners as well as newcomers who can bring fresh ideas to the campaign trail. They will act as the candidate's advocates and help handle every aspect of the campaign, from raising money to knocking on doors.

ASSEMBLING A TEAM

A candidate running for office, no matter how small, needs to bring on a campaign manager with experience working on political campaigns. The campaign manager generally possesses legal expertise and should be familiar with the laws and regulations of campaign oversight. Campaign managers oversee the operational aspects of getting the candidate elected. They implement strategy, attend to scheduling, coordinate staff and volunteers, conduct meetings, and handle paperwork. If anybody has a question, that person will ask the campaign manager. If an extra person is needed to stay late at headquarters or fill in at a campaign event, the campaign manager will arrange this.

Some experts, such as veteran political strategist Christine Pelosi, recommend against choosing a family member or close personal friend as a campaign manager. The campaign manager must maintain objectivity and be willing to give the candidate bad news about the campaign if necessary.

A campaign also includes staff members or volunteers who oversee specific aspects of the campaign. In a small campaign, a handful of people may take on multiple roles. In big campaigns, each specialist coordinates a team of staff and volunteers. The following are a few key roles in a political campaign:

A treasurer or finance director oversees fundraising and spending.

A public relations or communications director works to increase name recognition of the candidate and spread the campaign message via the media. The public relations director will also give advice on making a positive impression on voters.

A field operations manager mobilizes volunteers on the ground for efforts such as canvassing—knocking on voters' doors to talk about the candidate.

An office manager attends to correspondence, contacts volunteers, oversees campaign literature, and keeps records.

Larger campaigns have additional dedicated positions, such as scheduler, volunteer coordinator, fundraising director, social media or online operations director, house party coordinator, political director, database manager, and policy or research director. A campaign may also hire professional consultants to help shape the direction of the campaign. They may offer guidance and services related to handling the

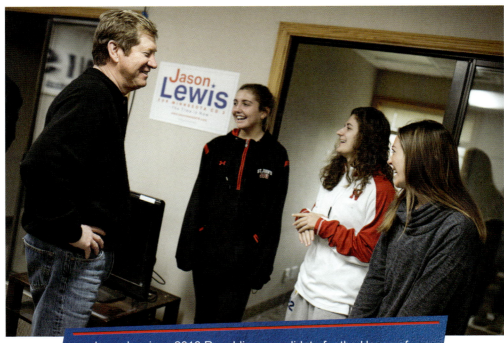

Jason Lewis, a 2016 Republican candidate for the House of Representatives in Minnesota, talks to volunteers in his campaign office during the run-up to Election Day.

media, plotting strategy, fundraising, public opinion polling, and online communications.

Enthusiastic volunteers are essential for any successful campaign. Candidates can start out by recruiting volunteers among family and friends, as well as from organizations with similar positions on issues. Volunteer sign-up sheets should be made available at house party fundraisers and other campaign events. Campaigns welcome teen volunteers, and teens may be given formal positions as interns or fellows. Some teens volunteer when the candidate is a family member or a friend of the family. Other times, teens become aware of a candidate's campaign through organizations such as clubs for young Democrats or Republicans.

Volunteering for a campaign can be a big commitment in terms of time and personal investment, and a candidate should consider volunteers to be a valuable resource. Candidates should provide effective training and assign volunteers to tasks that match their skills. Volunteer activities should be well organized— volunteers won't continue to show up if meetings always start late or if campaign materials aren't ready when they arrive.

GETTING ORGANIZED

A thorough campaign plan is essential to running a successful political race. The campaign plan incorporates strategy, goals, the candidate's message, and a timeline. In crafting a campaign plan, the team takes into account all of the knowledge and research about the voters and their priorities, the strengths and weaknesses of political opponents, the campaign's resources, and the roles of staff and volunteers in campaign activities. There are software programs that can be used to create a streamlined version of the campaign plan—major donors sometimes ask to see the campaign plan before making a commitment to support a candidate. A solid campaign plan demonstrates that the campaign is well organized and viable.

The campaign plan also encompasses the candidate's message, the theme of the campaign, and the general tone of campaign literature. The message provides the answer to the question, "Why are you running for office?" Candidates must also work to shape their image, in both ideological and practical terms. They will need to state their positions on key issues clearly and prepare a brief stump speech to serve as an introduction at public events. They will also have to consider matters such as appropriate clothes, demeanor, and public speaking ability. Making a good first impression can be crucial to winning over voters.

Campaign literature also gives candidates a means of introducing themselves to voters. This includes mailers, brochures, posters, and yard signs. Campaign literature is usually printed professionally, but candidates and their teams produce the content and approve the design. The candidate's website and social media outreach should also reinforce the campaign theme and message.

The campaign will also need to set up an office and quickly begin operations. For a small campaign, a home office in a supporter's house may be adequate. A larger campaign requires more space, ideally near the center of the candidate's district. The campaign

Campaign literature is displayed during Alexandria Ocasio-Cortez's kickoff rally for her 2018 congressional campaign, held in the Bronx, a borough of New York City.

plan should account for providing office furniture, technology, and supplies.

A well-organized campaign will succeed in moving seamlessly from the initial announcement into active campaigning. Daily routines will involve clerical work, contacting voters, fundraising, research, producing and distributing campaign literature, making progress reports, and holding meetings about strategy. No campaign unfolds exactly according to plan, but a solid campaign plan and strategy can adapt to unexpected developments on the campaign trail.

TWENTY-FIRST CENTURY CAMPAIGNING

Technological developments have transformed political campaigns. The rise of social media, new media, and grassroots activism facilitated by online tools have made it easier for ordinary people to come together at a local level to support campaigns through action and small donations. But this new connectivity has created a faster news cycle, requiring campaigns to speed up their operations.

In the twentieth century, campaigns tended to rely on personal knowledge and experience in crafting a campaign. Twenty-first century campaigners have access to big data and analysis of that data. Data analytics allow campaigns to target voters with personalized appeals based on sets of data obtained online. These practices, however, bring up privacy concerns for individuals.

New low-tech trends have also affected campaign strategy. Some states now allow early voting, either in person or by mail. These options make voting easier and more convenient, but they disrupt the typical campaign plan that includes a big get-out-the-vote drive just before Election Day.

Savvy political campaigners will adapt to the latest innovations. A successful campaign should strike a balance between innovative tactics and tried-and-true means of reaching voters.

CAMPAIGN OUTREACH

Once the campaign is underway, the team focuses on connecting with voters. A successful candidate runs a smart campaign, deploying volunteers and resources where they're most likely to be effective. The team may use data such as demographic statistics and voter files to identify and target voters who are likely to support the candidate if they receive a phone call or a visit from a volunteer. Specific circumstances in the ward and the campaign schedule will also determine day-to-day efforts. Early on, activities such as circulating the nominating petition, research, fundraising, and preparing campaign materials will take a higher priority. As Election Day nears, staff and volunteers will focus on a get-out-the-vote push.

Personal appearances by the candidate provide the most direct contact with voters. In a local race, community members may already know the candidate by sight or reputation. In addition to speeches, house parties held by supporters, and media events, the

Engaging the public is essential to connecting with voters. Here, Vermont gubernatorial candidate Christine Hallquist greets customers at a cafe in 2018.

candidate will put in appearances at civic functions, party events, and public gatherings such as fish fry dinners or local music festivals. Generally, the candidate is accompanied at these events by supporters who may hand out campaign literature or sign up volunteers.

Campaign staff members contact voters using the data in voter files, which often includes telephone numbers and addresses, and through information collected during the campaign. Volunteers are provided with a script on calls to voters to encourage them to vote, or, if it's a follow-up, perhaps to invite them to attend a candidate event. Campaigns also send out flyers through the mail urging residents to vote for the candidate.

The internet, social media, and text messaging enable campaigns to increase their outreach. The campaign website should have links to the candidate's social media accounts. Social media accounts that are active and engaging can be valuable for reaching voters and connecting with community leaders and local political figures. The candidate can share news from the campaign trail by posting photos and updates. Text messaging and email can provide a personal connection to supporters.

The candidate may also have allies among the political establishment, activist groups, other campaigns, and community leaders. These can be valuable sources of guidance and support. An official endorsement from an important political figure, respected organization, or key media outlet can give the campaign a big boost.

For many onlookers, the most visible form of campaigning is paid media, meaning ads on TV, the radio, digital platforms, billboards, and in newspapers. A local campaign probably won't have the budget for a huge media blitz, but the team can draw on research and experience to select the advertising options that will reach the highest number of likely voters.

Another valuable source of publicity is earned media, or news coverage of the candidate. This type of media can't be purchased. Gaining the attention of the media requires effort and persistence. A candidate can seek media exposure by issuing press releases, making public appearances, reaching out to reporters, and writing opinion pieces for publication. Supporters can write letters to the editor.

One of the most traditional and reliable means of reaching voters is through door-to-door canvassing. Volunteers are provided with maps and lists of names, and they knock on doors at those addresses. The candidate will probably do some canvassing personally as well. The primary goal of canvassing is to increase visibility and name recognition of the candidate. Volunteers talk about the candidate, answer questions, hand out campaign

Massachusetts State Senate candidate Dr. Katie McBrine (*right*) canvasses local houses with her campaign manager. A pediatrician, she made health care issues central to her platform.

literature, and ask if they can count on the voter's support. They make a note of the response so that the campaign team can track their progress toward the vote goal.

Volunteers should be nicely dressed and courteous. Even if the person answering the door is rude or confrontational, the volunteer should remain calm and polite. Volunteers should know the relevant laws about distributing campaign literature. There may be restrictions on when and where lawn signs can be displayed, for example, and it's illegal for campaign workers to put literature directly into mailboxes.

Canvassing is the most visible volunteer role in the campaign, but volunteers are busy behind the scenes as well. They may keep records, prepare mailers, and do research. They help plan, set up, and attend public events. They run errands, drive the candidate around, and arrange meetings. They're also essential for soliciting contributions and organizing fundraisers.

Teenage volunteers perform many of the same jobs as adult campaign volunteers, from entering data to handing out campaign materials. Like any other volunteer, they are expected to make a good impression on behalf of the candidate. The campaign may keep parents informed about their child's activities, and teens generally accompany an experienced canvasser when going door to door.

CHAPTER THREE

FINANCING THE CAMPAIGN

In most political campaigns, the candidate with more money wins the election. Even the best-qualified candidate, with a great platform and message, must achieve name recognition to win over voters. Potential contributors may not take a candidate seriously until the campaign has demonstrated that it can raise money and use it in ways that raise the candidate's profile.

Nonetheless, financial considerations shouldn't deter a determined novice candidate from launching a campaign. There are plenty of cases in which underdog candidates have won out over better-funded opponents. In addition, depending on the circumstances, a candidate may be able to avoid large-scale fundraising. In a small campaign, financial support from family, friends, and associates, as well as the candidate's own money, may be adequate to fund the race.

Some candidates may be eligible for public financing as well, depending on state and municipal laws. Typically, a candidate participating in a publicly

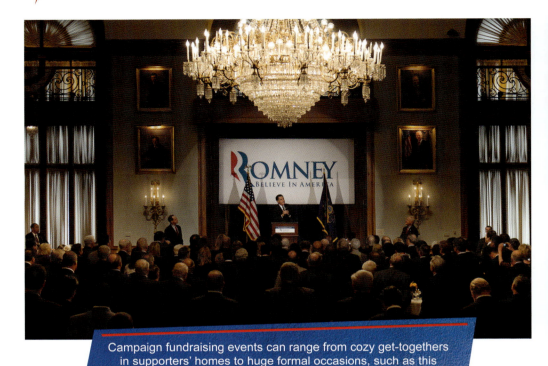

Campaign fundraising events can range from cozy get-togethers in supporters' homes to huge formal occasions, such as this 2012 fundraiser for presidential candidate Mitt Romney.

financed campaign accepts only small contributions from donors. The rest of the campaign's funding is provided by the public finance program, which may match the donations or provide the campaign with a set amount of money. The concept of public financing is intended to lessen the influence of big donors in politics. There is a limit on how much a publicly financed campaign can spend as well as possible restrictions on how public money can be used.

Regardless of how candidates decide to fund the campaign, they should be aware of the relevant laws and regulations. Candidates are required to file reports of their campaign income regularly, for example. There are limits on how much a single donor can give to a campaign. It's critical that a candidate follows the rules and maintains transparency when raising money. Even unfounded claims of campaign finance violations can tarnish a candidate's image.

FUNDRAISING

A fundraising plan should be included in the candidate's overall campaign plan. It should include the campaign budget, fundraising goals, and deadlines for campaign finance reporting. The campaign should draw up a list of possible donors and the means of reaching out to them.

Candidates new to politics often feel uncomfortable asking people for money. Veteran campaigners, however, will point out that candidates aren't requesting handouts. They are asking that the donor support their vision. A willingness to ask for money demonstrates that candidates believe strongly in their own message and are dedicated to making a difference in the community.

When coming up with a list of prospective donors, the campaign team should consider the various reasons people decide to give money to political causes. In his book examining political campaigns, *Political Campaigns: Concepts, Context, and Consequences*, Costas Panagopoulos identified three prominent types of donors. "Investors" prioritize their business interests, and they donate to candidates with views sympathetic to their business or industry. "Ideologues" donate to candidates with policy stances similar to their own. "Intimates" donate because of their personal relationship with the candidate or connections to the community.

Candidates should begin by considering how much they are personally willing to put into the campaign. Candidates often spend their own money or take out loans to help finance the campaign. The first people they ask for donations are family members and friends. They also ask people who belong to their business, social, and political circles; staff and volunteers do likewise. The campaign may have access to lists of donors who have given to other campaigns and causes with similar political stances. The candidate can contact local philanthropists and organizations. The local political party may support the campaign. However, candidates should also identify cases in which they might consider refusing a donation for ethical reasons.

Having money available to spend from the very beginning can provide early momentum for the campaign. Getting out a strong message from the start indicates to potential donors that the candidate has the resources and support to generate votes. This is the stage when money from the candidate's close circle can make a big difference.

Campaigns reach out to potential donors using a variety of tools. Direct mail solicitations include a letter of introduction from the candidate and a return envelope for contributions. Online fundraising includes making sure there are donation links on websites, ads, and social media sites, as well as email solicitations sent to a targeted list. Volunteers also call potential donors to ask them for a contribution or invite them to candidate events.

One of the most effective and widely used fundraising methods is "dialing for dollars"—phone call solicitations from the candidate or a top staff member. A

Candidates contact potential donors by mail, phone, email, and social media platforms. Here, volunteers at a phone bank make calls to voters for 2016 presidential candidate Ted Cruz.

campaign team sometimes spends hours a day making calls. When contacting a potential major donor with a fundraising solicitation, the candidate should always make the request personally.

Campaign events are another standard means of fundraising. Supporters invite potential donors to meet-and-greet events with the candidate, such as house parties or breakfast events with coffee and pastries. Attendees will meet the candidate and mingle with other supporters. They may give a donation, sign up to volunteer, or offer to hold their own event for the candidate. Larger campaigns often hold ticketed events, such as formal benefit dinners that include entertainment and a speech by the candidate. The event may incorporate a theme and include other fundraising tactics, such as a raffle.

The campaign should follow up with a thank-you note to donors to let them know that their contributions are valued. A personalized note signed by the candidate will make the best impression. The donors are also added to a mailing list so that they can receive campaign updates and another solicitation later on.

BIG MONEY AND SPECIAL INTERESTS

Many of these fundraising activities assume that prospective donors will primarily be people or organizations who give for personal or business reasons. But in some local races, candidates may benefit from "big money" donations that come from outside the community.

There are many different types of organizations that spend money to influence elections, either by donating to the candidate or independently advocating on their behalf. These special interest groups, which often support candidates based on their policy positions, are not always subject to the rules that regulate a candidate's own fundraising activities and finance reporting. Money raised by the campaign—hard money—is limited per donor, and the identity of the donors is disclosed. Money spent by outside groups can include soft money, which is not capped, and dark money, in which the donors can remain anonymous.

Political action committees (PACs) and super PACs are two types of these organizations. Many PACs represent the political interests of corporations or organizations such as unions. Others are the advocacy branches of groups interested in protecting certain

Prominent Republicans speak during the 2019 Conservative Political Action Conference (CPAC) in Maryland, held to promote a conservative political agenda.

rights or supporting a particular position on an issue. PACs can donate directly to political campaigns, subject to certain restrictions. The super PAC is a new type of group that was made possible by the 2010 Supreme Court decision in *Citizens United v. Federal Election Commission*. Super PACs can raise unlimited amounts of money to be used for political purposes, but they cannot contribute directly to political campaigns. There are also various types of

CAMPAIGN FINANCING AROUND THE WORLD

In general, the United States spends more money on its election campaigns than most other countries. According to a Library of Congress report comparing campaign finance restrictions in various countries, other countries are more likely to cap the amount of money candidates can raise or spend, limit political advertising, and provide public funding. In Austria, for example, presidential candidates and political parties are limited to spending € 7 million (about $8 million) per campaign. Canada caps campaign spending according to a formula calculated by election officials. Many countries restrict political advertising, especially on television, and instead allot free airtime for candidates to promote their messages. Examples of countries that do this include Belgium, France, and Great Britain. Norway leads in the proportion of public funding spent on elections, with 67 percent of all campaign funding coming from the government in 2017, according to Statistics Norway.

organizations that use dark money to influence the political process.

PACs, super PACs, and dark money groups primarily focus on national and state elections, but they may also spend their money to influence local elections. Candidates might receive contributions from PACs representing unions or super PACs backing issue advocacy organizations, for example. Dark money can play a role in local elections as well, such as in instances in which special interest organizations advocating for charter school expansion have used dark money to support candidates supportive of charter schools for city school board seats.

CAMPAIGN FINANCE REGULATIONS

For a novice candidate, campaign finance regulations can seem complex and intimidating. It's essential, though, that a campaign follows the regulations scrupulously and maintains transparency regarding how money is raised and spent. Violating the rules can result in legal consequences. Ethically questionable financial dealings could become an issue in the race, too. The city clerk or elections office can help a candidate comply with finance regulations.

In general, if a campaign intends to raise money above a certain limit, the candidate must establish

Michael Cohen, former lawyer for President Donald Trump, leaves a New York federal court in 2018 after pleading guilty to campaign finance violations and other charges.

an authorized campaign committee that takes in contributions. The treasurer of the campaign committee keeps records of all campaign contributions and expenditures as well as the identity of all donors. Contribution and expenditures forms must be filed with election administrators by certain deadlines. The treasurer should set up a reporting system early on in the campaign to avoid compliance violations.

There are restrictions on who can donate to a campaign. Organizations such as corporations, unions, and nonprofit groups cannot directly contribute to a candidate, but their PACs can give money. People who are foreign nationals can't donate to political campaigns. (It generally is legal for minors to make contributions, though, so an enthusiastic teenage volunteer is allowed to give to the campaign.) There are also caps on the amount of money a supporter can donate. Candidates, however, are generally not limited in making contributions to their own campaigns.

Candidates must take great care to keep personal, campaign, and government financial dealings separate. If candidates want to finance their own campaigns, the money must be transferred to the campaign committee. Campaign money cannot be spent on personal use—the candidate's day-to-day expenses not related to the campaign. A candidate also can't use government resources in a campaign. If the candidate already holds an elected office, for example, that person typically cannot use official stationery for campaign correspondence or conduct campaign activities in a public building.

CHAPTER FOUR

STAYING THE COURSE

Election season is often referred to as a slog, though it may seem more like a roller coaster to campaign staff. Workers will have to keep up their day-to-day fundraising and outreach activities while reacting to any unexpected developments. Often, a solid incumbent easily wins reelection, but novice candidates with little money or name recognition sometimes manage astonishing upsets.

In 2016, for example, twenty-one-year-old Florida Republican Amber Mariano became Florida's youngest state senator. She

Alexandria Ocasio-Cortez questions Michael Cohen during his appearance before a House committee on February 27, 2019, just months after she became the youngest woman ever elected to Congress.

37

won against a better-funded opponent who was favored to win in the polls. In 2018, New York Democrat Alexandria Ocasio-Cortez defeated veteran incumbent Joe Crowley in a primary election, taking office at the age of twenty-nine as the youngest member of the United States Congress.

WINNING OVER THE VOTERS

Every aspect of campaigning, from fundraising to holding rallies to canvassing, serves the ultimate objective of connecting with voters and earning their votes on Election Day. A candidate's priorities on the campaign trail reflect both the overall campaign strategy as well as day-to-day concerns. The campaign plan maps out shifting goals during different stages of the campaign, and the campaign is usually marked by certain milestones that have the potential to give the candidate a significant boost.

In some races, the candidate must win a primary election by defeating opponents from the same political party before advancing to the general election. Some districts hold closed primaries, in which only registered members of the candidate's political party can vote. Elsewhere, primaries are open to all registered voters. If none of the candidates receive 50 percent of the vote, there may be a runoff—a second primary election. In some cases, there may be only one strong candidate running from the party, and primaries are unimportant. In others, the primary results may essentially decide the election; if the district is solidly Republican or Democratic, the opposing party may not be able to compete.

A candidate may have to appeal to a different set of voters in the primary as opposed to the general election. The campaign staff will take this into account in planning strategy and allocating resources. After the primary, the winning candidate's former opponents (from his or her own party) generally express support for the victor in the general election.

A high-profile event covered by the media—such as a policy speech, press conference, or interview—can give the candidate valuable exposure to voters. The candidate should be well prepared both on the message and presentation. If the event is a speech, candidates might share stories about connecting with voters on the campaign trail. If it's a TV appearance, the candidate should know whether the interviewer is most likely to be interested in policy positions or in a human-interest aspect. For a candidate new to the campaign trail, public speaking may be difficult but it will grow easier with experience.

Candidates may also have a chance to distinguish themselves from opponents during events such as debates. Other common formats include town hall meetings or candidate forums. These events are often sponsored by civic organizations or local media outlets. A moderator, or sometimes members of the public, will ask candidates about their positions. Candidates should present themselves as confident, well informed, and in touch with the issues voters care about.

Endorsements can provide another major boost for a campaign. The endorsement of a member of the political establishment or a newspaper, for example, demonstrates confidence in the candidate's abilities. An endorsement from a labor union or community leader shows that they believe the candidate is working for the constituents' best interests. Endorsements improve candidates' name recognition and enhance their reputation.

Candidates for the office of New York City public advocate participate in a forum in 2019, in which they discussed issues such as AIDS prevention and housing.

In bigger races, results of public opinion polls indicate voters' views of candidates. Good numbers in polls can help maintain a campaign's momentum. They confirm that the campaign's strategy is working and that the message is effective.

HANDLING SETBACKS AND MAINTAINING INTEGRITY

A political campaign almost never goes completely smoothly. A campaign may stumble when the candidate has trouble gaining name recognition, money runs low, or polling numbers are worrisome. Any

GETTING OUT THE YOUTH VOTE

Election turnout of voters under thirty years old generally lags behind other age groups. In *Get Out the Vote*, authors Donald P. Green and Alan S. Gerber describe a school-based First-Time Voter Program that educates high school seniors about voting and encourages them to register to vote. A volunteer discusses the political process with a group of students and describes why voting is important. Then they practice voting on a voting machine of the type used in their district. An evaluation of the First-Time Voter Program found that voter turnout among participants was 10 percentage points higher than among students who didn't attend—an impressive improvement.

There are many organizations that use similar approaches to encourage young adults to vote. If you're passionate about promoting civic participation among your friends and classmates, research whether you can get involved with any such programs in your area or online. Such efforts are generally nonpartisan—you can't stump for your favored candidate—but you can encourage your peers to learn about the candidates and issues in making their choices.

Attendees at a music festival sign up to resister to vote. The group HeadCount encourages political participation among music fans by registering voters at concerts.

of these outcomes could lead to a change in campaign strategy. But for many candidates, the most difficult aspect of the campaign is when the tone of the race turns negative.

In a negative campaign, candidates seek to improve their position by attacking their opponent. Attacks might be directed at an opponent's political positions, voting record, or business dealings. They may draw unfavorable attention to people or groups who have endorsed the opponent or donated to the campaign. Sometimes, attacks dig into the candidate's personal life or spotlight an unintentional gaffe on the campaign trail. The candidate may reveal an embarrassing incident from the opponent's past, which can be particularly damaging if there are photographs. Sometimes, a smear campaign involves half-truths or even outright lies. A campaign may reinforce a negative message by emphasizing the same damaging point over and over again, in the hope that voters will come to associate the opponent with the negative content.

Candidates have to be wary, however, of public backlash against campaigns smearing the opponent. Super PACs and other outside groups are more likely to launch negative attacks than a candidate's own campaign because they don't have to worry about alienating voters.

When candidates are the target of negative campaigning, they must decide how to handle it. Many candidates begin a campaign intending to avoid negativity. When their opponent turns to mudslinging, however, it may seem like the attacks will hurt their chances at winning unless the campaign responds.

A campaign should plan for the possibility of negative attacks from the start. Candidates and their teams should be ready to counter any negative claims and refocus attention back on the campaign's message. Handling a negative attack capably can make a good impression on voters.

Candidates sometimes decide that they will counter with a negative claim of their own only if it is relevant to the opponent's fitness for public office. For example, campaign contributions and expenditures are generally made public. The media as well as campaigns on both sides will monitor filings to check for mistakes or irregularities. If the opponent is an incumbent who oversees zoning, it would be fair for a candidate to point out a conflict of interest if the opponent accepts donations from real estate developers.

ELECTION DAY

The final days before the election bring a final push to get out the vote. Many voters remain undecided until late in the campaign. Volunteers canvas the precinct, make phone calls, and register voters. The campaign may hold a rally and arrange to offer rides to voters on Election Day. The candidates and campaign team will reiterate their message on issues the voters care about.

On Election Day, the candidates may give an interview in which they thank the team, thank voters, and make a final appeal for votes. The campaign may assign poll watchers to the polling places where people vote. Poll watchers observe the election and point out any irregularities or errors. They may also track who has voted so that the campaign staff can call up supporters

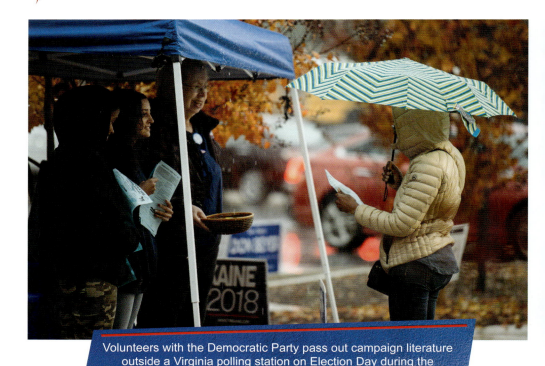

Volunteers with the Democratic Party pass out campaign literature outside a Virginia polling station on Election Day during the 2018 midterm elections.

who haven't been to the polling place and urge them to vote. Poll watchers are not allowed to campaign or intimidate voters. Often, campaign volunteers will hand out literature outside the polling place, although laws require that they stay a certain distance away.

On the evening of Election Day, the campaign staff generally throws a postelection party. Even if the candidate loses, this is the time that staff and volunteers will be able to celebrate their efforts and feel like they've accomplished something worthy. At this event, the candidate will make a final appearance to declare victory or announce concession to the opponent.

CHAPTER FIVE

LOOKING AHEAD

Working on a political campaign can be an empowering and edifying experience. After the election is over, staff and volunteers may decide to devote their newly gained expertise to fresh causes and endeavors.

Regardless of whether the candidate won or lost, the campaign will want to review and assess the strengths and weaknesses of the campaign. Did the message resonate with voters? Were there any setbacks that could have been avoided with better planning or organization? Was the communications strategy a success? Did the candidate sufficiently mobilize volunteers and supporters? Did the campaign raise adequate funds for a competitive run?

The candidate who lost the election will usually call the opponent on election night to offer congratulations. The campaign winds down and pays its remaining bills. The candidate will reflect on what comes next, whether

Campaign staffers look on as Jack Graham, a Republican Senate candidate in Colorado, gives a concession speech in 2016 following his loss during the primary election.

it's trying for another elected office in the future or serving the community in another way.

PUBLIC OFFICE

If the candidate won, the next stage is making the transition to office. Most local governments provide resources such as training seminars to introduce new officeholders to the everyday responsibilities of an elected official. There are regulations, protocol, and official duties to learn. Depending on the office, the official may need to set up an office and hire staff.

Newly elected members of the 116th Congress pose in front of the US Capitol in Washington for their "freshman" class photo on November 14, 2018.

Supporters will expect elected officials to carry out campaign promises after they take office. However, elected officials must work in the interests of all constituents, not just the people who voted for them during the election. They must provide leadership and put effort into every aspect of the job.

Once in office, the official will become acquainted with other officeholders as colleagues. Some will be allies in their positions on the issues, while others will hold opposing views. In order to achieve their objectives, newly elected officials will have to network with colleagues who have opinions on both sides of the issue. Reaching a resolution will require negotiation and compromise.

Legally, campaign activities must be kept separate from public duties, but elected officials should still stay in touch with their supporters. They can keep their supporters updated on accomplishments, initiatives, community news, and services available to constituents.

MAKING A DIFFERENCE

Participating in a political campaign can provide valuable experience relevant to activism work and public service. Unsuccessful candidates may realize that, despite the loss, they have a flair for political work and may pursue political campaigning or consulting as a career. A volunteer with extensive political campaigning experience might consider seeking a paid position in a future campaign. A campaign worker with a flair for policy or administrative expertise might seek a job in government. Candidates who win their election sometimes hire campaign workers as staff members in their office.

Teen volunteers often say that working on a political campaign helps boost their confidence and expand their awareness of the issues they feel passionate about. Some campaign activities take teens out of their usual comfort zone, such as initiating conversations with prospective voters or asking strangers for money over the phone. Teen volunteers often receive the same training as adults, and they need to employ top-notch communication skills and make a good impression on the public during their campaign work. When

CAMPAIGN FINANCE REFORM

In 2018, $5.7 billion was spent on the midterm elections, according to OpenSecrets.org. This amount was exceeded only by the 2016 and 2012 elections, which each topped $6 billion. In the 2018 election, small contributions given by individuals made up only about 16 percent of this amount.

To many voters, the huge amount of money given by wealthy special interest groups represents a threat to democracy. In order to compete, candidates are forced to appeal to big donors, raising the likelihood that they will craft their message to attract special interest groups rather than ordinary citizens. Once in office, legislators are more likely to approve policy that favors their wealthy donors.

Some people and groups have called for measures curbing the influence of special interest groups in politics. Increased transparency and disclosure requirements would provide voters with more information about big donors. Donors supporting campaigns or funding issue-based ads with dark money would be unable to hide their identities. Public funding could also be strengthened to give more influence to small donors. If small donations were matched or even exceeded by public funds, candidates might devote more effort to drawing support from ordinary voters.

An activist protesting the influence of money in politics holds up a sign during a 2016 demonstration calling for reform of voting laws and campaign finance.

volunteering for a political campaign, teens learn a lot about the political system as well as skills that can be applied to other activities. Expertise in organizing events, raising money, and articulating policy, for example, can be assets when it comes to activism and community organizing work.

Twenty-first century teen activists have become key figures in social movements. As a fifteen-year-old advocate of girls' education in Pakistan, Malala Yousafzai was shot and nearly killed for her activism

Greta Thunberg (*center*) marches in a climate change protest in Hamburg, Germany, in 2019. Thousands of students in the city walked out of school and marched to demand action on climate change.

work in 2012. She was awarded the Nobel Peace Prize in 2014 and continues to champion human rights. The high school students of Parkland, Florida, transformed the discussion of gun control in the United States after the horrific 2018 mass shooting in their school. Young climate activists such as Greta Thunberg have energized young people to act on the issue of climate change; the fifteen-year-old Swedish girl spoke before the United Nations during a climate conference in 2018.

If you're passionate about making a difference, you

don't have to set out to change the world. Start by looking for public service opportunities in your community. Volunteer work can be a great way to connect with diverse people from your community and learn more about the everyday issues residents are concerned about. If you became an advocate for a particular cause during your work on a political campaign, you might consider raising awareness in your community. If you believe strongly that the voting age for teens should be lowered to sixteen, for example, start by getting

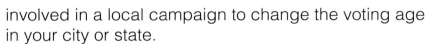

involved in a local campaign to change the voting age in your city or state.

If you're fascinated by the political process and want more hands-on experience, consider getting involved in student government or youth city councils. You'll confront many of the same challenges as a candidate running for public office, from learning about the issues voters care about, to creating a platform, and generating enthusiasm for your candidacy. Many people who eventually go on to run for public office report that they participated in student government in school. Whether you win or lose, it could be great experience for the next time you work on a political campaign.

GLOSSARY

ballot A list of candidates running for office; the process by which voters mark their chosen candidates during elections.

campaign A process by which candidates try to appeal to voters to win their support in an election.

campaign finance All funds intended to promote candidates, policy, or political parties. Laws regulate how that money can be used in elections.

candidate Someone who runs for public office.

canvas The process of systematically soliciting votes during a campaign, often by going door-to-door to encourage constituents to vote.

constituent A voter who lives in a district represented by an elected official.

democracy A system of government in which all eligible people vote for elected officials to represent them in government.

district A geographic area defined for administrative or electoral purposes.

endorsement Official public approval or support, usually from an influential person or organization.

expenditure Funds that have been spent, which must be disclosed on financial reporting forms.

fundraising Asking for money for a specific purpose, such as a charity or a political campaign.

incumbent A person currently holding elected office.

nonpartisan Not associated with a specific political party.

opponent Someone competing against another person, as in a contest or political race.

partisan Associated with a specific political party.

political action committee (PAC) A political committee that raises money and donates it to political candidates or causes.

politician Someone who is professionally involved in politics, often serving as an elected official.

primary election An election held in advance of the general election in which voters choose which candidate receives the political party's nomination.

turnout The number of people who vote in an election.

union An organized group of workers formed for the purpose of protecting and advancing their interests.

volunteer Someone who willingly provides work without being paid.

Campaigns & Elections
(202) 644-9008
Website: https://www.campaignsandelections.com
Facebook: @CampaignsandElections
Twitter: @C_and_E
Campaigns & Elections is a publication focusing on all
   aspects of political campaigning.

Canada World Youth
2330 Notre-Dame Street West, Suite 300
Montreal, QC, H3J 1N4
Canada
(514) 931-3526
Website: http://canadaworldyouth.org
Facebook: @CanadaWorldYouth.JeunesseCanadaMonde
Twitter: @cwyjcm
Canada World Youth is a nonprofit organization that
   provides youth the opportunity to gain leadership
   skills through its international volunteer program.

Center for Information & Research on Civic Learning
   and Engagement (CIRCLE)
Jonathan M. Tisch College of Civic Life
Tufts University
Lincoln Filene Hall
10 Upper Campus Road
Medford, MA 02155
(617) 627-3453
Website: http://civicyouth.org
Facebook: @Center-for-Information-Research-on-Civic
   -Learning-and-Engagement-CIRCLE

Twitter: @CivicYouth
CIRCLE helps increase civic engagement of young
    people and works to change policy that affects
    marginalized youth.

Elections and Democracy
Elections Canada
30 Victoria Street
Gatineau, QC K1A 0M6
Canada
(800) 463-6868
Website: https://electionsanddemocracy.ca
Facebook: @DemocracyCA
Twitter: @democracyCA
Created by Elections Canada, Elections and
    Democracy is a civic education program intended
    to educate students about participating in the
    democratic process.

Indivisible
Email: contact@indivisible.org
Website: https://indivisible.org
Facebook: @indivisibleguide
Instagram: @indivisibleteam
Twitter: @IndivisibleTeam
Indivisible is an activist nonprofit group that promotes
    and supports progressive grassroots organizations,
    candidates, and policies.

National Democratic Institute (NDI)
455 Massachusetts Avenue NW, 8th Floor
Washington, DC 20001
(202) 728-5500

Website: https://www.ndi.org
Facebook: @National.Democratic.Institute
Instagram: @ndidemocracy
Twitter: @NDI
The National Democratic Institute is a nonprofit
　　organization that supports democratic institutions
　　worldwide by promoting government accountability,
　　safe elections, and civic participation.

Youth Service America (YSA)
1050 Connecticut Avenue NW, #65525
Washington, DC 20035
(202) 296-2992
Website: https://ysa.org
Facebook: @youthserviceamerica
Twitter: @YouthService
Youth Service America is a nonprofit organization that
　　promotes service, learning, and leadership among
　　young people through community activism.

Donovan, Sandra. *Media: From News Coverage to Political Advertising*. Minneapolis, MN: Lerner Publishing Group, 2016.

Duffy, Claire. *The Teen's Guide to Debating and Public Speaking*. Toronto, ON: Dundurn, 2018.

Hosein, Ann. *Political Science*. New York, NY: Rosen Publishing, 2016.

Hurt, Avery Elizabeth. *Women in Politics*. New York, NY: Rosen Publishing, 2018.

Landau, Jennifer. *Teens Talk About Leadership and Activism*. New York, NY: Rosen Publishing, 2018.

Lansford, Tom. *Corruption and Transparency*. Broomall, PA: Mason Crest, 2017.

Machajewski, Sarah. *Political Corruption and the Abuse of Power*. New York, NY: Greenhaven Publishing, 2019.

Moyle, Eunice. *The Future Is in Your Hands*. Lake Forest, CA: Walter Foster Jr., 2018.

Perkins, Anne. *Trailblazers in Politics*. New York, NY: Rosen Publishing, 2015.

Santos, Rita, ed. *Gerrymandering and Voting Districts*. New York, NY: Greenhaven Publishing, 2019.

Small, Cathleen. *Diversity in Politics*. New York, NY: Rosen Publishing, 2019.

BIBLIOGRAPHY

Green, Donald P., and Alan S. Gerber. *Get Out the Vote: How to Increase Voter Turnout*. 3rd ed. Washington, DC: Brookings Institution Press, 2015.

Grey, Lawrence. *How to Win a Local Election: A Complete Step-By-Step Guide*. Lanham, MD: M. Evans, 2007.

Johnson, Dennis W. *Campaigning in the Twenty-First Century: Activism, Big Data, and Dark Money*. New York, NY: Routledge, 2016.

Lawless, Jennifer. *Becoming a Candidate: Political Ambition and the Decision to Run for Office*. New York, NY: Cambridge University Press, 2012.

Library of Congress. "Regulation of Campaign Finance and Free Advertising." November 2, 2018. https://www.loc.gov/law/help/campaign-finance-regulation/index.php.

Litman, Amanda. *Run for Something: A Real-Talk Guide to Fixing the System Yourself*. New York, NY: Atria, 2017.

Mariano, Amber, as told to Tess Koman. "I Got Rejected from Harvard. Then I Won a State Election." *Cosmopolitan*, October 10, 2017. https://www.cosmopolitan.com/politics/a12252792/amber-mariano-florida-state-representative.

Mark, David. *Going Dirty: The Art of Negative Campaigning*. Lanham, MD: Rowman & Littlefield, 2009.

Nwanevu, Osita. "I Ran for Office and Won: Four First-Time Candidates Explain How." Slate, January 16, 2017. https://slate.com/news-and-politics/2017/01/i-ran-for-office-and-won-heres-how.html.

OpenSecrets.org. "Election Overview." Retrieved February 18, 2019. https://www.opensecrets.org/overview.

Panagopoulos, Costas. *Political Campaigns: Concepts, Context, and Consequences*. New York, NY: Oxford University Press, 2017.

Pelosi, Christine. *Campaign Boot Camp 2.0: Basic Training for Candidates, Staffers, Volunteers, and Nonprofits*. San Francisco, CA: Berrett-Koehler, 2012.

Rosen, Linzy. "Why I Volunteer for Political Campaigns." *Teen Vogue*, October 1, 2018. https://www.teenvogue .com/story/why-i-volunteer-for-political-campaigns.

Scher, Richard K. *Political Campaigns in the United States*. New York, NY: Routledge, 2016.

Shaw, Catherine. *The Campaign Manager: Running and Winning Local Elections*. 6th ed. New York, NY: Routledge, 2018.

Simpson, Dick, and Betty O'Shaughnessy. *Winning Elections in the 21st Century*. Lawrence, KS: University Press of Kansas, 2016.

Statistics Norway. "Political Parties' Financing." September 13, 2018. https://www.ssb.no/en/partifin.

Strauss, Valerie. "Dark Money Just Keeps on Coming in School Board Races." *Washington Post*, October 29, 2017. https://www.washingtonpost.com/news/answer -sheet/wp/2017/10/29/dark-money-just-keeps-on -coming-in-school-board-races.

Watts, Jonathan. "'The Beginning of Great Change': Greta Thunberg Hails School Climate Strikes." *The Guardian*, February 15, 2019. https://www.theguardian .com/environment/2019/feb/15/the-beginning-of-great -change-greta-thunberg-hails-school-climate-strikes.

Williamson, Melanie. *How to Run for a Political Office and Win: Everything You Need to Know to Get Elected*. Ocala, FL: Atlantic Publishing Group, 2012.

ABOUT THE AUTHOR

Corona Brezina is an author who has written numerous young adult books for Rosen Publishing. Several of her previous books have focused on legal and social issues concerning teens, including *Personal Freedom and Civic Duty: Understanding Equal Rights* and *Standing Up to Bullying at School.* She lives in Chicago.

PHOTO CREDITS

Cover Hero Images/Getty Images; pp. 4–5 (background graphics) weerawan/iStock/Getty Images; p. 5 Stephen Maturen/Getty Images; pp. 8, 40 Pacific Press/LightRocket/Getty Images; p. 10 © AP Images; pp. 13, 28 The Washington Post/Getty Images; p. 15 Robert Nickelsberg/Getty Images; pp. 18, 47 Tom Williams/CQ Roll Call/Getty Images; p. 21 Don Emmert/AFP/Getty Images; p. 23 Stephanie Keith/Getty Images; p. 25 The Boston Globe/Getty Images; p. 31 Jim Watson/AFP/Getty Images; p. 33 SOPA Images/LightRocket/Getty Images; p. 35 Drew Angerer/Getty Images; p. 37 (inset) Mandel Ngan/AFP/Getty Images; p. 41 Taylor Hill/Getty Images; pp. 44, 49 Andrew Caballero-Reynolds/AFP/Getty Images; p. 46 Helen H. Richardson/The Denver Post/Getty Images; pp. 50–51 Axel Heimken/AFP/Getty Images; additional graphic elements moodboard - Mike Watson Images/Brand X Pictures/Getty Images (chapter opener backgrounds), Maksim M/Shutterstock.com (fists).

Design and Layout: Michael Moy; Editor: Rachel Aimee; Photo Researcher: Nicole DiMella